WARRIORS HAVE WOUNDS

A Strange Journey of Change

E. Amoako

Codelitemedia

I dedicate this book to everyone who would break a glass ceiling.

"And would they not let him know that he had gone up but only in order to come back down into the cave with his eyes ruined- and thus it certainly does not pay to go up". Plato-Allegory of The Cave.

For Hilary & Roy

The Lord is with you, mighty warrior.
Judges 6:12 NIV

The Author,

[signature]

Immanuel

CONTENTS

Title Page	
Dedication	
Foreword	
chapter 1	1
CHAPTER 2	4
CHAPTER 3	8
CHAPTER 4	11
CHAPTER 5	15
CHAPTER 6	19
CHAPTER 7	22
CHAPTER 8	26
CHAPTER 9	30
CHAPTER 10	34
CHAPTER 11	37
CHAPTER 12	40
CHAPTER 13	44
conclusion	47
bibliography	48
Acknowledgement	49
About The Author	51

FOREWORD

There is a well known phrase 'what doesn't kill us make us stronger.' Sometimes when life throws us challenges, it can feel like there is no way that things will ever get any better for us. In his debut book, Emmanuel Amoako shares with us the stories of 12 people who when faced with adversity did not give up. Reading about these very different warriors give hope; when life gives you lemons make lemonade. The prominent message that the hard things we face can shape the people we become. We do have the strength to overcome adversity, and the people who we meet in the book demonstrate just that. We are warriors. We have wounds. This book is a celebration of the power that this creates, and an inspiration for us all.

Lucy Clarke,
Community advocate & Social Prescribing Administrator.

CHAPTER 1

WARRIORS HAVE WOUNDS

We have ordinary people who have overcome great battles and remain standing not broken and weak but instead stand stronger, joyful and more alive than ever.

The wounds they carry as a result of these battles is a reminder of their tenacity, audacity, relentlessness and ambition.

Warrior

The oxford dictionary defines a warrior as a brave fighter.

It is very possible to win the war and at the same time lose some battles.

BBC TV and radio presenter Victoria Derbyshire describes the hair loss she suffered during cancer treatment as the worst part of her illness. She won the fight against cancer, and lost her hair.

In the second world war (1939-1945), the allied powers led by Britain, France, US, Soviet Union and China lost several battles. For instance, in the Battle of Crete, the Mediterranean island was lost to the Axis forces. They also lost the Battle of Corregidor which culminated in the Japanese conquest of the Philippines. Overall however, the Allied powers were the victors of the second world war.

So one can win the war and however loss some battles; mental battles, emotional battles, moral battles, religious battles, even legal battles.

◆ ◆ ◆

So when Emmeline Pankhurst decided that enough was enough and that women should be allowed to vote in Britain, she co-founded a group with the motto 'deeds and not words'.

Known as the suffragettes, they undertook a series of uncompromising protests which led to her several spells behind bars, episodes of force-feeding and a lot of trouble with the authorities. Eventually in 1928, men and women got the same voting rights, thanks to their activism.

With the price, comes the prize!

The battle ground is in our minds, hearts, conscience, imagination, our bodies, our souls.

The combat range is in the present, past and also the future.

Some are fighting for the future.

When there is intrusion into the private lives of heirs, heiresses, princes and princesses it is because they are going to be future Kings and Queens. The battle is about the future.

Some people are fighting inherited battles, battles passed from previous generations.

◆ ◆ ◆

Martin Luther King Jr said, "I have a dream".

It is my aspiration that people begin to bear with one another. There are many gallant individuals who are carrying wounds.

Some wounds are physical, others are emotional, some social and some mental. Others have healed and carrying scars.

There is however a victory that comes by the comfort, direction and power that hope provides during adversity.

This book is a collection of the inspiring stories of ordinary individuals who broke the glass ceiling.

From explorers, writers, artists, leaders, activists, scientists, nuns and entrepreneurs.

It is possible!!

CHAPTER 2

NELSON MANDELA

Rolihlahla Mandela was born on 18 July, 1918 in South Africa into the Madiba clan in the village of Mvezo, in the Eastern Cape.
Hearing the elders' stories of his ancestors' valour during the wars of resistance, he dreamed also of making his own contribution to the freedom struggle of his people.

He attended primary school in Qunu where his teacher, Miss Mdingane, gave him the name Nelson, in accordance with the custom of giving all schoolchildren "christian" names.

He was a freedom fighter who became South Africa's first black president.

Fun Fact

There's a woodpecker named after him

From Cape Town to California, streets named after Mandela abound. But he's also been the subject of some rather unusual tributes. Scientists have named a prehistoric woodpecker after him: *Australopicus nelsonmandelai*. In 1973, the physics institute at Leeds University named a nuclear particle the 'Mandela particle.'

Famous Quotes

> *"Do not judge me by my successes, judge me by how many times I fell down and got back up again".*

> *"It always seems impossible until it's done."*

> *"Many people in this country have paid the price before me and many will pay the price after me."*

Apartheid

This was a system of institutionalised racial segregation that existed in South Africa and South West Africa (now Namibia) from 1948 to the early 1990s.

For instance, it was deemed illegal for citizens to marry across racial lines and places of residence and housing were determined by race.

Life And Politics

In 1952 Mandela was the deputy president of the African National Congress – a party determined to overthrow the racist apartheid regime in South Africa. After state police killed 69 black activists in 1960, the ANC and Mandela with it, agreed to reprisal attacks on state facilities like rail and power lines in protests during which lives were lost.

He was arrested in 1962, and sentenced to life in prison.

From 1964 to 1982 Mandela was incarcerated at the brutal Robben Island Prison, off Cape Town. He also had spells at the maximum-security Pollsmoor Prison and subsequently at Victor Verster Prison near Paarl.

He endured long stints of solitary confinement, often going without sleeping or toilet facilities – tested and proven torture methods designed to reinforce prisoner's sense of powerlessness. All together he spent 27 years in prison.

Yet the opposite happened. Mandela became the focal point for a global campaign against apartheid.

Release

On February 11, 1990, the South African government under President de Klerk released Mandela from prison. Shortly after his release, Mandela was chosen deputy president of the ANC; he became president of the party in July 1991. Mandela led the ANC in negotiations with de Klerk to end apartheid and bring about a peaceful transition to non-racial democracy in South Africa.

In April 1994 the Mandela-led ANC won South Africa's first elections by universal suffrage, and on May 10 Mandela was sworn in as president of the country's first multi-ethnic government.

Mandela wasn't removed from the US terror watch list until 2008 – at age 89. He and other members of the African National Congress were placed on it because of their militant fight against apartheid.

He Drew His Inspiration From A Poem

While he was in prison, Mandela would read William Ernest Henley's "Invictus" to fellow prisoners. The poem, about never giving up, resonated with Mandela for its lines "I am the master of my fate. I am the captain of my soul."

Legacy

Once Mandela was elected president in South Africa's first free elections in 1994 he did not seek retribution, despite his brutal prison treatment. Instead, he governed for the whole country, arguably preventing a civil war.

The Truth and Reconciliation Commission, which aimed to heal South Africa through confession and forgiveness rather than revenge, was established during his time in office. It has since been used as a model for other countries.

The autobiography Long Walk to Freedom, which chronicles his early life and years in prison, was published in 1994.

His body was abused but his mind remained free, Nelson Mandela's sacrifice helped defeat apartheid.

CHAPTER 3

FRANKLIN D. ROOSEVELT

Franklin Roosevelt was born on January 30, 1882 in Hyde Park, New York, United States.

He is America's longest serving president, also the first with a significant physical disability. The 32nd President of the United States, he remains the only US President to serve for more than two terms.

Franklin D. Roosevelt was diagnosed with polio in 1921 and had to use a wheelchair from the age of 39 – with his most politically active years ahead of him. Known for building up strength in his upper body, it was said of Roosevelt that he lifted himself from a wheelchair to lift a nation from its knees.

Fun Fact

Franklin Delano Roosevelt was an avid collector.

Roosevelt had a life-long love affair with postage stamps. He started collecting them as a child and later attended stamp shows, bought rarities from stamp dealers, and joined stamp clubs. He even designed a few stamps himself. "I owe my life to my hobbies—especially stamp collecting," FDR once remarked.

Famous Quotes

> "Inequality may linger in the world of material things, but great music, great literature, great art and the wonders of science are, and should be, open to all."

> "We have always known that heedless self-interest was bad morals; we know now that it is bad economics".

> "The only limit to our realization of tomorrow will be our doubts of today".

Life And Politics

On August 9, 1921, 39-year-old Franklin D. Roosevelt, at the time a practicing lawyer in New York city, joined his family at their vacation home. On August 10, after a day of strenuous activity, Roosevelt came down with an illness characterized by fevers, ascending paralysis, facial paralysis, prolonged bowel and bladder dysfunction, numbness and hypersensitivity of the skin.

Roosevelt came close to death from the illness, thought to be Guillain–Barré syndrome in contemporary diagnosis. Most of the symptoms resolved themselves, but he was left permanently paralyzed from the waist down.

Legacy

FDR was inaugurated as US president in March 1933. That month the country recorded over 15 million unemployed (25% of the total workforce) and banks across America were closing owing to the 1929 stock market crash. This was the Great Depression.

Roosevelt instituted a 100-day plan, to be called the New Deal. It turned the economy around and transformed America into a superpower.

He devoted much thought and planning to the body that would become the United Nations after the second world war in 1945.

Whiles in Office, he instigated an extraordinary fund-raising campaign called the March of Dimes which kick-started the 20th century's largely successful eradication of polio, worldwide.

Although dealing with this crippling disease was difficult, many believe that his personal struggles helped shape Franklin D. Roosevelt, both as a man and as a president.

CHAPTER 4

MOTHER TERESA

"Saintly giver of comfort to the destitute"

Mother Teresa was born Agnes Gonxha Bojaxhiu on August 26, 1910 in Skopje, North Macedonia. Saint Teresa of Calcutta (known as Mother Teresa) was an Albanian-born Indian Roman Catholic missionary and nun who devoted her life to helping those most in need.

She founded the Missionaries of Charity in India in 1950, and for over 45 years, she ministered to the poor, sick, orphaned and dying.

Fun Fact

Mother Teresa Had Multiple Nationalities

While much of Mother Teresa's charitable work began in India, she considered herself to have multiple nationalities. Her family was of Albanian descent. She herself was born in Skopje, in the then Ottoman Empire. Following her charitable work in India, she adopted Indian citizenship. When asked to describe her nationality, she said, "By blood, I am Albanian. By citizenship, I am Indian. By faith, I am a Catholic nun. As to my calling, I belong to the world. As to my heart, I belong entirely to the heart of Jesus."

Famous Quotes

"Peace begins with a smile."

"Let no one ever come to you without leaving better and happier. Be the living expression of God's kindness: kindness in your face, kindness in your eyes, kindness in your smile."

"If you judge people, you have no time to love them."

Life

At the age of twelve, she felt strongly the call of God. She knew she had to be a missionary to spread the love of Christ. At the age of eighteen she left her parental home in Skopje and joined the Sisters of Loreto, an Irish community of nuns with missions in India. After a few months' training in Dublin she was sent to India, where she lived most of her life. On 4th September 2016, she was canonised by the Catholic Church as Saint Teresa of Calcutta. The anniversary of her death, 5 September, is her feast day.

"The Call Within A Call"

From 1931 to 1948 Mother Teresa taught at St. Mary's High School in Calcutta, but the suffering and poverty she glimpsed outside the convent walls made such a deep impression on her.

While traveling on a train from Calcutta to the Himalayan foothills for a retreat, Teresa experienced what she later described as "the call within a call." The idea that all people are God's children gripped her, and she heard Jesus telling her to quit her teaching to help those most in need by living amongst them.

Inspired by Jesus' words in the Gospel, "I was hungry and you gave me food, I was thirsty and you gave me drink, I was a stranger and you welcomed me," Mother Teresa worked to serve "the poorest of the poor" on the streets of Calcutta. She gave away all of her possessions and lived in dire poverty with them in hopes of being better able to serve them.

Although she had no funds, she depended on divine providence, and started an open-air school for slum children. Soon she was joined by voluntary helpers, subsequently financial support came making it possible for her to extend the scope of her work.

She spent her life caring for the poor.

Although Mother Teresa displayed cheerfulness and a deep commitment to God in her daily work, her letters (which were collected and published in 2007) indicate that she did not feel God's presence in her soul. She also alluded to lacking the earlier zeal that had characterised her efforts to start the Missionaries of Charity

The letters reveal the suffering she endured and her feeling that Jesus had abandoned her, especially at the start of her mission. Continuing to experience a spiritual darkness, she came to believe that she was sharing in Christ's Passion, particularly the moment in which Christ asks, "My God, my God, why have you forsaken me?"

Despite this hardship, Mother Teresa integrated the feeling of absence into her daily religious life and remained committed to her faith and her work for Christ.

Legacy

At the time of her death aged 87 in 1997, she ran over 500 missions in over 100 countries, including hospices and homes for people with HIV/AIDS, leprosy and tuberculosis. Also soup kitchens, family and children's counselling programs, orphanages and schools.

Mother Teresa served those who were most vulnerable and made many sacrifices in order to help others. She devoted her life to serving those in need without judgment.

CHAPTER 5

WALT DISNEY

Walter Elias Disney was born on December 5, 1901, in Chicago, Illinois.

Disney was an American artist, animation film producer and entrepreneur.

He founded the entertainment conglomerate the Disney Company, regularly ranked among the top 50 companies in America.

Fun Fact

Walt Disney played Peter Pan in a school play.

The story Peter Pan surely held a special place in Walt Disney's heart: not only was it a hit movie for him in 1953, it also took him back to his childhood. After seeing Peter Pan on stage, young Walt was given the opportunity to play the Boy Who Wouldn't Grow Up in a school performance. Walt later recalled that his brother Roy was in charge of the rope used to hoist him over the stage to simulate flying; it was just one of their many creative collaborations.

Famous Quotes

"If you can dream it, you can do it"

"The way to get started is to quit talking and begin doing."

"It's kind of fun to do the impossible."

Life And Work

Walt Disney began his first series of fully animated films in 1927, featuring the character Oswald the Lucky Rabbit. When his distributor appropriated the rights to the character, Disney altered Oswald's appearance and created a new character that he named Mortimer Mouse; at the urging of his wife, Disney rechristened him Mickey Mouse.

Disney was rejected loans for Micky Mouse by bankers over 300 times because they thought the idea was "absurd". The irony is that one of the 20th Century's most creative visionaries was actually fired for lacking creativity from his local newspaper many years before.

In 1934 Disney began work on his first feature-length animated film: Snow White and the Seven Dwarfs, one of the first-ever projects to prove animation's capacity for long-form narrative.

Snow White was quickly followed by Pinocchio, Dumbo, Bambi, and Fantasia—and the opening of a new studio in Burbank to keep up with the demand for new releases.

After that feat of changing the world of film forever, Walt Disney moved to his next big project: Disneyland, a California theme park that opened in 1955.

However, "The Happiest Place On Earth" was not an easy or clear road to success.

The parks would have never seen the light of day had Disney not persevered after 300 rejections from financiers for the Mickey Mouse concept that started this incredible journey.

Disney World in Orlando has now grown to become the largest single-site employer in the U.S. The Disney Group of companies posts annual incomes above $50 billion.

Walt Disney Felt Responsible For His Mother's Death.

Once he became successful, Walt bought his parents a rather extravagant present: a new house. And when his parents needed something fixed, tweaked, or repaired, he sent his own repairmen from the studio over to take care of it.

Such was the case when they discovered a problem with their furnace in 1938. Tragically, his team didn't take care of the issue properly, and his mother Flora Disney died of carbon monoxide poisoning at the age of 70. His father, Elias, also fell very ill from the gas leak, but survived. Walt's daughter, Sharon, said that even years later, Walt found the subject nearly impossible to talk about.

CHAPTER 6

FLORENCE NIGHTINGALE

She was born on 12 May 1820 in the Italian city of Florence, after which she was named. The second daughter in a prominent and wealthy British family, growing up it was clear Florence was devoted to serving others. As a teenager, she would spend time helping the sick and poor in the village near her family estate and believed nursing was her calling.

She is best known as the first professional nurse and founder of modern nursing.

Fun Fact

During her work in the Crimean War, Florence would nurse soldiers at night. She would carry a lamp with her during her rounds which would lead to her nickname "Lady with the Lamp." She grew to be a person of fame as people were captivated by the lady who walked around with the lamp.

Famous Quotes

"It may seem a strange principle to enunciate as the very first requirement in a hospital that it should do the sick no harm."

"I think one's feelings waste themselves in words; they ought all to be distilled into actions which bring results."

"I attribute my success to this: I never gave or took any excuse."

Life And Work

She aspired to serve others, in particular, she wanted to become a nurse. Her parents were opposed to her aspirations as at that time, nursing was a menial labour not seen as attractive or 'respectable'.

Florence was determined to fulfil her dream of becoming a nurse and she paid lots of visits to hospitals and health facilities to find out more.

Her parents eventually allowed her to study nursing for four months at the Kaiserwerth Deaconesses' Institute, a Lutheran Hospital of Pastor Fliedner in the city of Düsseldorf in Germany.

❖ ❖ ❖

In Victorian Britain, wealthy women like Florence weren't

expected to work – daily life was spent seeing to servants, entertaining guests, reading, sewing and attending social events. But Florence saw something very different for her future. Florence later wrote that she felt suffocated by the vanities and social expectations of her upbringing.

Legacy

She found a training school for nurses and in (1859) she wrote Notes on Nursing. This became a standard reference book for those entering the nursing profession and also the general public who wished to learn basic techniques.

With her guidance, nursing became a profession.

She inspired nursing in the American Civil War, and in 1870 trained Linda Richards, who returned to the US where she developed the nursing profession in America.

CHAPTER 7

MARIE CURIE

Marie Curie, née Maria Sklodowska, was born in Warsaw Poland on November 7, 1867, the daughter of a secondary-school teacher. She received a general education in local schools and some scientific training from her father.
Marie Curie became one of the most important scientists of her generation. Her discoveries enabled the development of modern radiation and X-Ray, paving the way for a new era of cancer treatment.

Fun Fact

Her notebooks are radioactive. Marie Curie died in 1934 of aplastic anemia (likely due to so much radiation exposure from her work with radium). Marie's notebooks are still today stored in lead-lined boxes in France, as they were so contaminated with radium, they're radioactive and will be for many years to come. Radium, after all, has a half life of 1,600 years.

Famous Quotes

> " We must have perseverance and above all confidence in ourselves. We must believe that we are gifted for something and that this thing must be attained."

> "Nothing in life is to be feared; it is only to be understood."

> "Be less curious about people and more curious about ideas."

Life And Work

Though a top student at school, Curie was not allowed to attend the men-only University of Warsaw in her hometown; nor was there an alternative place for women to learn.

Curie faced significant prejudice and discrimination as a woman and as an immigrant, throughout her career.

For instance, despite winning an unprecedented second Nobel Prize, she was never admitted to the all-male French Academy of Sciences.

Scientific Discovery

In 1902 Marie isolated radium (as radium chloride), determining its atomic weight as 225.93. The journey to the discovery had been long and arduous and involved dangers the Curies did not appreciate.

Her early researches, together with her husband, were often performed under difficult conditions, laboratory arrangements were poor and both had to undertake much teaching to earn a livelihood.

During the time of research, they began to feel sick and physically exhausted. Today we can attribute their ill-health to the early symptoms of radiation sickness. At the time they persevered oblivion to the risks, often with raw and inflamed hands because they were continually handling highly radioactive material.

Curie coined the term 'radioactivity'. Her research with her husband Pierre also led to the discovery of two previously unknown elements: polonium and radium.

In 1906, Curie's husband Pierre Curie was killed in a traffic accident, leading Marie to continue their research alone. She took over Pierre's teaching post at Paris' Sorbonne University and in 1914 founded the Radium Institute to find medical applications for radioactivity.

During the First World War, Marie bought and operated portable X-ray machines to help treat wounded soldiers on the frontline.

Legacy

Curie's pioneering research inspired a generation of women in science and medicine who followed in her footsteps spurred on by Curie's remarkable accomplishments, passion for research and perseverance.

Such was Curie's commitment to her research that her death in 1934 of aplastic anaemia was caused by exposure to radiation.

In 1995, Marie and Pierre Curie were reburied in the Pantheon – the Paris mausoleum reserved for France's most revered dead – on the orders of French President Mitterand.

CHAPTER 8

J.K. ROWLING

Joanne Rowling was born on 31 July 1965 at Yate General Hospital near Bristol, and grew up in Gloucestershire in England and in Chepstow, Gwent, in south-east Wales. She became the world's best-selling children's author, despite managing on benefits as a single mother.

Initially, her manuscript for Harry Potter was rejected by several publishers.

Fun Fact

Her prized possession is a set of first-edition of Jane Austen novels that she keeps near her at all times.

Famous Quotes

"I have never been remotely ashamed of having been depressed. Never. What's to be ashamed of? I went through a really rough time and I am quite proud that I got out of that."

"Talent and intelligence never yet inoculated anyone against the caprice of the fates."

"There is an expiry date on blaming your parents for steering you in the wrong direction; the moment you are old enough to take the wheel, responsibility lies with you."

Life And Work

J.K. Rowling is a British author of the much-loved series of seven Harry Potter novels, originally published between 1997 and 2007. She is also a philanthropist.

She adopted her pen name, J.K., incorporating her grandmother's name, Kathleen, for the latter initial. Rowling does not have a middle name.

Her childhood was generally happy, although she does remember getting teased because of her name, "Rowling" – She recalls often getting called "Rowling pin" by her less than ingenious school friends. J.K. Rowling says she never really warmed to her own name.

In 2011, she gave testimony to the Leveson enquiry about how some news reporters sought to intrude into her family's privacy. After her books became best-sellers, reporters would often be camped outside her home.

J.K. Rowling said:

"However, as interest in Harry Potter and myself increased, my family and I became the target of a different kind of journalistic activity. The effect on me, and our family life, truly cannot be overstated. We were literally driven out of the first house I had ever owned because of journalists banging on the door, questioning the neighbours and sitting in parked cars immediately outside the gate. Old friendships were tested as journalists turned up on their doorsteps, and offered money for stories on me. "(J.K.Rowling's Testimony to Leveson Enquiry Nov 2011.)

After finding a letter from a journalist in her child's satchel, she remarked:

"It's very difficult to say how angry I felt that my 5-year-old daughter's school was no longer a place of complete security from journalists."

J.K. Rowling currently lives in Scotland, on the banks of the River Tay, with her 2nd husband Neil Murray; J.K. Rowling has three children, two with husband Neil.

Honours & Awards

J.K. Rowling has received many honours and awards, including:

Companion of Honour, for services to literature and philanthropy, 2017
PEN America Literary Service Award, 2016
Freedom of the City of London, 2012
Hans Christian Andersen Award, Denmark, 2010
Chevalier de la Legion d'Honneur: France, 2009
Lifetime Achievement Award, British Book Awards, 2008

CHAPTER 9

VINCENT VAN GOGH

Vincent Van Gogh was born on March 30, 1853 in Zundert in southern Netherlands, the son of a pastor.

While Vincent van Gogh is one of the art world's most renowned painters, he is also synonymous with the term 'tortured artist'. Ignored in his lifetime, poorly understood by the Beaux-Arts and ill-appreciated by his contemporaries, Van Gogh profoundly disrupted painting conventions, leaving a lasting legacy and close to 900 artworks.

His most expensive artwork, Orchard with Cypresses, sold for $117.2 million at Christie's New York in 2022.

Fun Fact

Although his last name is most commonly pronounced "van go", it is actually pronounced "van gokh."

Famous Quotes

"I dream my painting and I paint my dream"

"I often think that the night is more alive and more richly coloured than the day"

"Great things are done by a series of small things brought together."

Life And Work

Aged 15, in 1869, he took his first job, working in The Hague branch of an international art dealing firm.

Van Gogh's job took him to London and Paris, but he was not interested in the work and was dismissed in 1876. He briefly became a teacher in England, and then, deeply interested in Christianity, a preacher in a mining community in southern Belgium.

In 1880, at the age of 27, he decided to become an artist. He moved around, teaching himself to draw and paint and receiving financial support from his younger brother Theo. In 1886, Van Gogh joined Theo in Paris, and met many artists including Degas, Toulouse-Lautrec, Pissarro and Gauguin, with whom he became friends. His style changed significantly under the influence of Impressionism, becoming lighter and brighter.

In 1888, Van Gogh moved to Provence in southern France, where he painted his famous series 'Sunflowers'. He spent time in psychiatric hospitals and swung between periods of inertia, depression and incredibly concentrated artistic activity, his work reflecting the intense colours and strong light of the countryside around him.

He Painted Almost 900 Paintings In 10 Years

Up until van Gogh was 27, he had explored several different jobs – he'd been a lay minister, teacher and art dealer.

Suddenly, he abandoned these careers and decided to focus all his energy on painting and drawing.

Over the next ten years, van Gogh went on to create a body of work which included almost 900 paintings, and a further 1,100 works on paper.

Van Gogh Lived With Mental Illness Throughout His Life

His symptoms included hallucinations, depression, and seizures – which at times were quite severe.

Many modern day psychiatrists have attempted to diagnose his illness from the symptoms he showed, and possible diagnoses include schizophrenia, bipolar disorder, syphilis, hypergraphia, Geschwind syndrome, and temporal lobe epilepsy. It is also quite possible that he had a combination of these.

As van Gogh's mental health was often poor, he spent a lot of time in and out of hospital.

'Starry Night' Was Created In Psychiatric Hospital

This artwork sold for $50 million in 1990. It is still highly esteemed and keeps increasing in value.

Luckily for van Gogh, while he was in hospital he could continue creating his art – and he would spend the days looking through the barred windows at the scenery below. It was here he completed his most famous work: 'Starry Night'.

Starry Night shows his view on different days, and even at different times of day. As he sat and watched the light and weather change, he painted the view at sunrise, moonrise, on sun-filled days, overcast days, windy days and rainy days.

Van Gogh Was A Pioneer Of The Post-Impressionistic Selfie

Over a period of three years, van Gogh painted an impressive 43 self-portraits – but it had less to do with vanity than necessity.

As he struggled to afford paid models and had a limited social circle, van Gogh simply had few other people to paint.

His other cost-saving tricks included painting over his artworks instead of buying new canvas which makes you wonder what else could be hiding under those 900 paintings.

Only 37 years old when he died and having only sold one painting, van Gogh did not live long enough to see the extent of his legacy – which includes his works now being some of the most expensive in the world.

CHAPTER 10

EMMELINE PANKHURST

Emmeline was born on July 14, 1858 in Manchester, England and brought up in a politically active family. Known for Suffragette and champion of woman suffrage whose 40-year campaign for women's vote in Britain achieved complete success in the year of her death.

Fun Fact

Emmeline changed her birthday date.

She was born on the 14th of July, 1858 in Moss Side, Manchester. As per the birth register, it was written 15th of July, the same year.

It is possible that she changed to 15th for it marks the French Revolution. The revolution had its resonance with themes of equality.

Famous Quotes

> "We have to free half of the human race, the women, so that they can help to free the other half"

"I would rather be a rebel than a slave."

"It is obvious to you that the struggle will be an unequal one, but I shall make it - I shall make it as long as I have an ounce of strength left in me, or any life left in me."

Activism

After the campaign for women's right to vote had been (politely) running for decades Emmeline Pankhurst decided enough was enough. She co-founded a group with the motto "Deeds not words". This band of women became known as the suffragettes and Pankhurst led them through a series of uncompromising protests.

She believed winning the vote would never be achieved by constitutional means. She was imprisoned on a number of occasions for militant action, and went on hunger strike protests.

Her call for supporters to "rush parliament" saw her sent to prison for the first time.

Even behind bars the suffragettes strived to improve things. They objected to the conditions prisoners endured with a series of hunger strikes, many of which were brutally ended with force-feeding.

Legacy

When the First World War broke out and men headed for the battlefields, she encouraged women to step up and keep the country running – and they did. When the war was over calls for women's suffrage could no longer be ignored and in 1918 the

Representation of the People Act granted votes to all men over the age of 21 and women over the age of 30.

Pankhurst died on June 14, 1928, only a few weeks before the Representation of the People Act (1928) extended the vote to all women over 21 years of age.

Pankhurst's autobiography, My Own Story, appeared in 1914.

CHAPTER 11

HELEN KELLER

Helen was born in West Tuscumbia, Alabama on June 27 1880. She was left both blind and deaf at nineteen months as a result of what the doctors then called "brain fever" (possibly scarlet fever in modern terms). Most famous for her personal triumph over the limitations of both blindness and deafness, Helen Keller was one of the twentieth century's leading advocates for individuals with disabilities.

She was a writer, journalist, activist, ambassador, deaf, blind… Helen Keller's life was defined by what she could do.

Fun Fact

Helen Keller wrote to eight Presidents of the United States and received letters from all of them—from Theodore Roosevelt in 1903 to Lyndon B. Johnson in 1965.

Famous Quotes

"Optimism is the faith that leads to achievement. Nothing can be done without hope and confidence"

"Life is either a daring adventure or nothing at all."

"Character cannot be developed in ease and quiet. Only through experience of trial and suffering can the soul be strengthened, vision cleared, ambition inspired, and success achieved."

Growing Up

As a small child, she was viewed as unteachable and left to run wild, her inability to communicate prompting frequent rages. Reading of the Perkins School for the Blind's success with another deaf-blind girl, her parents ultimately asked the school to send Helen a teacher. Thanks to the pioneering work of 20-year-old teacher Anne Sullivan, herself partially blind, Keller learnt to read and write going on to graduate from University.

Activism

Keller wrote a best-selling – still in print – autobiography, contributed to newspapers, gave speeches and toured the world discussing everything from women's rights to atomic energy.

Keller's writing and activism did much to raise awareness of disability around the globe at a time when a lack of rights and unequal treatment of disabled people was common.

In 1924, she became the official spokeswoman for the newly formed American Federation for the Blind; she would serve in this role for the rest of her life. Keller's work helped profoundly alter the public's perceptions about individuals with disabilities.

Legacy

Confounding prejudice and changing attitudes, the way she lived her life helped disabled people the world over.

In 1999 her name appeared on Time magazine's list of the 100 most important figures of the 20th century, alongside such iconic figures as Albert Einstein, Franklin D. Roosevelt and Mahatma Gandhi.

CHAPTER 12

ERNEST SHACKLETON

He was born on February 15, 1874 in Kilkea, County Kildare in southern Ireland, but grew up in London.
He was a polar explorer and pioneer who led the famous 'Endurance' expedition.

Shackleton joined the merchant navy when he was 16 and worked on many different ships. He was an adventurer, who became interested in exploration and joined the Royal Geographical Society while still at sea.

His Ship Endurance, became hopelessly trapped in pack ice.

Shackleton abandoned one cherished goal and shouldered another, forced on him by circumstance. Through extraordinary hardships that lasted almost two more years, he ensured the survival of all 27 crewmen.

Fun Fact

Ernest Shackleton testified at the Titanic inquiry.

After returning from his second Antarctic trip, Shackleton was considered a leading expert in polar phenomena. For that reason, he was called to testify at the hearing following the sinking of the *Titanic* in 1912. The explorer delivered his opinion on the conditions that would have made the North Atlantic iceberg difficult for the navigators to see until it was too late.

Famous Quotes

"Difficulties are just things to overcome, after all."

"To be brave cheerily, to be patient with a glad heart, to stand the agonies of thirst with laughter and song, to walk beside death for months and never be sad – that's the spirit that makes courage worth having."

"Optimism is true moral courage."

Life And Work

He made three expeditions to the Antarctic, most famously in 1914 on the Endurance.

In 1901 he got a place on Captain Robert Falcon Scott's first Antarctic expedition but Shackleton's fellow explorers were forced to send him home on a supply ship due to bouts of illness.

The British National Antarctic Expedition considered him unfit for duty after the incident so he began raising money to mount his own missions starting him on his path as an independent explorer.

Purpose Of Shackleton's 1914 Antarctic Expedition

In 1914, in command of a party on the ship Endurance, Shackleton set off to cross the Antarctic from one side to the other, from the Weddell Sea to the Ross Sea.

As both Amundsen (a Norwegian explorer) and Scott (another British Antarctic explorer) had reached the South Pole and the Americans had reached the North Pole, he saw this as the last great challenge.

After the ship got trapped in the ice and eventually sank, they were all left stuck on a vast bit of ice for over two months. Shackleton and his crew escaped in lifeboats to the tiny Elephant Island. At the time, it was uninhabited and inhospitable, eerily 800 miles away from South Georgia, the nearest inhabited island.

He decided to leave most of the party behind, while he and five others set out on a smaller vessel to find help.

Everyone On The Team Rescued

Without the modern aids of radios, GPS, emergency helicopters or aerial reconnaissance Shackleton achieved the near impossible. They were all rescued

All the men believed that their survival was due largely to his tremendous leadership.

One of Ernest Shackleton's contemporaries Sir Raymond Priestly, Antarctic Explorer and Geologist famously commented,

"For scientific discovery give me Scott; for speed and efficiency of travel give me Amundsen; but when disaster strikes and all hope is gone, get down on your knees and pray for Shackleton.".

On January 5th, 1922, Sir Ernest Shackleton died suddenly of a heart attack. He was 47 years old. Alexander Macklin, one of the physicians from the Endurance who continued to serve Shackleton, wrote that the death was a result of "overstrain during a period of debility".

CHAPTER 13

LUDWIG VAN BEETHOVEN

Baptized December 17, 1770 Bonn, archbishopric of Cologne [Germany].

A German composer and pianist, his music is a testament to the unwavering human spirit in the face of cruel misfortune.

Widely regarded as the greatest composer who ever lived.

He was the predominant musical figure in the transitional period between the Classical and Romantic eras.

Fun Fact

He was bad at Math

He left school at age 11, after learning how to add and subtract, but before learning how to multiply or divide. To his last day, if he had to multiply say 60 * 54, he'd lay out 60, 54 times and add them up.

Famous Quotes

> "I will take fate by the throat; it will never bend me completely to its will."

"There are many princes and nobles. There is only one Beethoven"

'A great poet is the most precious jewel of a nation'

Life And Music

From the age of 25, Beethoven's hearing failed, generally attributed to some form of childhood illness. At 46, he became completely deaf and was unable to conduct an orchestra.

However, he continued to compose until his death in 1827, at the age of 56. During these ten years, he managed to compose some of the most beautiful works in his repertoire. Example the 9th symphony and his late string quartets, the Missa Solemnis.

Beethoven's deafness was not just a personal tragedy; it was also a professional and creative challenge that he desperately sought to overcome.

In the early 19th century, medical understanding of hearing loss was still in its infancy, and treatment options were limited. His deafness did not prevent him from composing music.

He also went through a rather long legal battle for custody over his nephew, Karl.

Despite suffering far-reaching medical ailments, emotional torments and family issues he is one of the most revered figures in Western Music.

In 1802 he wrote the emotional letter "Heiligenstadt Testament", where he expressed his determination to 'seize fate by the throat' and to continue ploughing through his work and life. He told of his deteriorating hearing.

The letter meant for his brothers Carl and Johann, was not posted.

There are several recorded episodes of anger, paranoia and fits of rage that plagued Beethoven's family, social and business relationships during this period. These episodes have mainly been attributed to the stress, frustration and misunderstandings caused by his hearing loss which he did well to hide for fear of not been invited to performances and shows.

In April and May 1814, playing in his Archduke Trio, Beethoven made his last public appearances as a soloist. The composer Louis Spohr noted: "the piano was badly out of tune, which Beethoven minded little, since he did not hear it …

Selected Beethoven Classics

Symphony No.3 in E flat, op.55 – 'Eroica' Symphony

Symphony No. 9 in D minor, op. 125 – 'Choral

String Quartet No.14 in C sharp minor, op.131

Symphony No. 5 in C minor, Op. 67

Violin Concerto in D, op.61

CONCLUSION

It seems to me that the scale, intensity and perplexity of one's battles in life is an indication of the nobility of the prize at stake.

we fall.

we break.

We fail.

but then,

we rise.

we heal.

we overcome.

--END.

BIBLIOGRAPHY

jkrowling.com/about

waterstones.com/blog/jk-rowling-harvard-speech-quotes

parliament.uk/about/living-heritage/Emmelin-pankhurst

goodreads.com/author/quotes/5840159.Emmeline_Pankhurst

npg.si.edu/learn/classroom-resource/helen-keller

goodreads.com/author/quotes/7275.Helen_Keller

smithsonianmag.com/smart-news/

catholic.org/clife/Teresa

mothernurselove.com/nightingale

natgeokids.com/florence-nightingale

motiva.art/blog/vincent-van-gogh-quotes

bbc.co.uk/history/icons

britannica.com/nelson-mandela

aruma.com.au/uncategorized

forbes.com/jamesasquith

wikipedia.org/roosevelt

mariecurie.org.uk/about

https://shackleton.com/blogs/articles/shackleton-quotes

https://www.goodreads.com/author/quotes/40589.Ludwig_van_Beethoven

ACKNOWLEDGEMENT

The poem the Road Not Taken by Robert Frost is a great inspiration. Not only does it have a personal connection to the story of my life but it also sums up in its own way the concept of any journey of change.

I also acknowledge my good friends Francis Mandela and Isabella of Isycreative.
Special mention also of Oldham Unity project and Revive Ministries.

Special thanks to Lucy Clarke for writing the foreword.

ABOUT THE AUTHOR

Emmanuel Amoako

E. Amoako is the founder and C.E.O. of Codelitemedia Group, owners of The Principal online news.

He is based in Oldham, United Kingdom where he is also involved with some charities and several community projects.

Printed in Great Britain
by Amazon